Rethinking Shame and Honour

THE M-SERIES is a collection of short, accessible papers and articles from Micah Global, being developed in response to the need for clear, authoritative statements on key themes. They form a foundation of historical and current ideas that contribute to our understanding and practice of integral mission. They aim to promote reflection, dialogue, articulation and action on the major concepts and issues that move us towards transforming mission.

The M-series is an essential resource for practitioners, theologians, students, leaders, and teachers.

M-Series from im:press

Titles in print:

Integral Mission: Biblical foundations
by Melba Maggay

The Five Marks of Mission: Making God's mission ours
by Chris Wright

Rethinking Shame and Honour
by Arley Loewen

In preparation:

Paying the Unpaid Debts by Flip Buys

Rethinking Shame and Honour

Arley Loewen
Leadership Training, Operation Mercy

Copyright © Arley Loewen

The author asserts the moral right
to be identified as the author of this work

Published by

im:press

An imprint of Micah Global

ISBN: 978-0-9945911-4-2

All rights reserved.

No part of this book may be transmitted or reproduced in any form or by any means, including but not restricted to photocopying, recording, or by any information storage and retrieval system, without written permission from the publisher; except for brief quotations in printed reviews.

Cover design: Tania Lubett

Typeset in Warnock Pro

Printed and bound by Ingram Spark

Foreword

*Therefore if anyone is in Christ, that person is a new creation:
The old has gone, the new is here!* (2 Corinthians 5:17)

As we encounter Christ and submit to him as our Lord and Saviour, we need to ask the tough questions of how should we now behave and live. Our values, cultural traditions, actions and words are to be placed before God, as we invite him to transform us, so that we can be his ambassadors, his servants, demonstrating his Kingdom.

Arley Loewen explores the honour and shame culture through the eyes of those who have been informed by it. He helps us to reflect together by drawing on examples and asking probing questions, inviting us into the transforming journey with Christ. Leadership in all its forms comes under the scrutiny of God's transforming love.

Rethinking Shame and Honour is an important addition to our Micah Series (M-Series). We encourage discussions and discernment as you read and work through the questions and reflections.

Courage for change!

Sheryl Haw
International Director of Micah Global

Introduction

No-one notices me!

IMAGINE walking into a room where three of your friends are having tea. However, none of them acknowledges your presence. They just continue their conversation as if you weren't there. You feel embarrassed and want to hide, wondering why you came. Then one of the friends looks at you, your eyes meet, he smiles and with a nod, invites you to join them. Warmth floods through you. You belong, you feel human: that small face-to-face connection has breathed life into your being.

I wish no-one would notice me!

My little granddaughter loves to play hide-and-seek with me. She tells me to count to ten, so she can run and hide. I pretend to look for her everywhere and then find her lying on our bed, a pillow covering her face. When her face is covered, in her world, she has become hidden. Amazing creativity—she even plays this game in the car.

But then a stranger meets my granddaughter, looks at her and asks her a question. She feels shy and looks away. She may actually cover her eyes, again thinking she is invisible and that no-one can see her.

This is not just a children's game. For adults it's very serious. Sometimes we may feel like others don't recognise our face, metaphorically. Sometimes, when we blush or are ashamed, we wish people would **not** recognise our face. That is why children sometimes cover their eyes, and why adults wear emotional masks—we are prone to hiding our 'face'.

English speakers refer to 'saving face' when meaning 'keeping honour' and not losing dignity or pride. And so we struggle with gaining and keeping face. As humans, we need honour. We cannot truly honour God, nor have positive relationships with one another, if we live in shame.

Those of us who are pastors of a church or managers of a project, sometimes say that we work for the glory of God. If we are honest, we want our ministry to bring honour to us as well. And of course, we want honour for and in our family. That is not a bad thing.

Without honour, we can't be effective leaders. Here are some thoughts to ponder as we move into our discussion.

- How can we gain honour?
- What do we need to do, so that those in our organisations or teams will honour us?
- Why do we sometimes do dishonourable things in order to maintain our honour?
- Why does our struggle for a 'good name' often lead to relational problems?

In this booklet we will explore how God has bestowed honour on humans. We will discuss characteristics of honour and shame. The main focus of this study will be on the challenges of gaining honour — how we sometimes resort to dishonourable ways to maintain our honour. This becomes false honour. We will look at honourable ways to gain and maintain true honour in church life, in mission and development projects, and in the family.

God honours humans

Honour at Creation

At creation, God crowned humans with glory and honour (Psalm 8:5). As God's noble creation, humanity carried a mandate to be God's representatives over the rest of creation. We bore His image (Genesis 1:26). We had real face, true honour.

Fallen into shame

But the first humans wanted more honour, almost as if they wanted to take God's place (Genesis 3:5). Instead, they experienced horrific shame (Genesis 3:7). They fell short, before God and one another. The world fell into sin and shame.

Ever since that fall into shame, people have tried to regain honour, but this constantly ends up as false or counterfeit honour. Humans worship and serve themselves, rather than the Creator (Romans 1:25).

We boast about how good we are. We gossip about how bad others are, tearing down their honour so we can have more. We abuse, hate and fight. We often shame others or boast in our group superiority, and even manufacture honour in order to cover ourselves. These are attempts to promote honour for ourselves or to take the honour from others.

God enters our story

When we look at the broader story of the Bible, we see an amazing story of good news.

God entered the garden to talk with Adam and Eve, even after they had shamed God by wanting His glory for themselves (Genesis 3:8-9). God honoured Abraham with a mandate to bless the entire world and to care for all peoples (Genesis 12:1-3). God entered Moses' story to save the people of Israel from bondage in Egypt (Exodus 3). God entered the world of Israel by directing them to build a tabernacle where He could dwell and meet with His people (Exodus 26-40).

Ultimately, God entered our world, as "the Word became flesh and dwelt among us" (John 1:14). In the Messiah, God ultimately honoured humankind. He entered our story, our lives.

Jesus saw the multitudes and had compassion on them (Matthew 9:36). He healed the sick and loved them. Jesus' story of the two sons reflects how the father honoured his own shamed sons by entering their lives (Luke 15). Finally, Jesus voluntarily offered His own life to carry our shame and restore dignity to every human being. We become Jesus' sisters and brothers, bearing a new name.

Transformed honour

But this is much more than a formal adoption into the divine family. The gospel of grace moves us from the competition for honour towards new honour. Boasting is cancelled (Romans 3:27). Esteeming others replaces jealousies (Philippians 2:3-4). Grace creates a fresh humility, allowing us to embrace criticism and overcome failure.

This is God's salvation story. Set in a world of honour and shame, this message connects with the values of many societies, especially those in the Global South.

As we revel in this new honour, we learn to do what God has done to us. As God loved us, so we now love and honour others.

Characteristics of honour-shame cultures

Strengths

When I have honour, it means I have **value** in my community. I matter to others. If I am a pastor with honour, I will have **influence**; people will pay attention to what I say. As a parent, my children will look up to me and ensure that I can hold my head up high in society. If I am a shopkeeper with honour, people will buy from my store. As the manager of an NGO project, government officials will heed my proposals much easier if I carry respect. And of course, the project staff will be more likely to implement the project if I, as their leader/boss, carry weight.

Having true honour can give me tremendous **freedom** to actually live above and beyond myself. I have a cause that goes beyond just myself. I sacrifice my own desires for the sake of my family. I live for the good name of the project. And above all, I will live for the honour of God and the people of God.

When I live for honour, I am able to truly **serve** others because I am no longer occupied with my own affairs. I consider my community as more important than myself.

Honour means **respect**. When I have honour, others respect me and I respect them. I guard their reputation and they guard mine. We are careful not to destroy others. Shame becomes an internal 'security force' that keeps us from doing shameful deeds.

> *Having a good reputation is like a fragile glass which I hold in my hands. If it falls, it will shatter*

Having honour from the community means I **belong** to a family and a larger community. I am connected to the past, to my ancestors. As a group, we have hope for the future, because our children and grandchildren continue to carry our name.

Dilemmas

At the same time, the need for seeking honour and avoiding shame is fraught with dilemmas and challenges.

When I am always thinking of what others will say, I have to look over my shoulder. I am **afraid** people may criticise me or even reject me. Having a good reputation is like a fragile glass which I hold in my hands. If it falls it will shatter forever, almost impossible to regain.

When someone violates my sense of honour, I feel compelled to protect my face. If I don't enact **revenge** and respond in violence, others will say I am weak.

Because honour comes from one's community, I will follow the traditions of my community. In contrast to individualism, I don't have an opinion of my own, but am **bound by the court of my group**. This means that I may ignore what I consider personally honourable or moral, in order to please the community.

Because I am so concerned about my public image, what happens when I do make **mistakes or fail**, which people would see as being shameful? I will naturally be reluctant to reveal any type of weakness. This easily leads to a double life—the public and the private life. And so we veil our problems, weaknesses and sins.

The struggle to gain and maintain honour often leads to **mistrust and suspicion**. Because we hide our inner or private worlds, we wonder what the other person is *really* thinking. We become obsessed with 'reading between the lines.'

To talk about
- What other strengths do you see in living by honour?
- What other dilemmas have you experienced in your struggle to avoid shame?

Challenges of leadership in shame and honour contexts

We want to raise our families with honour. Every pastor wants to lead their church with dignity. A director needs to lead their organisation with their head held high. But at times, we engage in dishonourable habits in order to keep our honour. How can we move towards a transformed honour, in our families, churches and organisations? Is it possible to gain honour in an honourable way? This is true, transformed honour.

New status in Jesus

> *Mani had come to faith in Jesus, and was growing in his new life. He enjoyed his college studies, but struggled with a lack of confidence. Being small in height, he sensed others looking down on him. He shared his insecurity with his Christian mentor. The two had established a deep friendship on-line, but had never met face-to-face. When the mentor learned Mani was only 130 cm tall, he laughed, "Guess what, Mani. I am smaller than you, but because the one I believe in and follow is above everyone else, no one can look down on me."*

The mentor, also new in faith, had experienced a new status in Jesus.

Needing status

Humans naturally want to have good status, so that they can enjoy more value, respect and honour from others. The higher my status (rank, position, standing, station) the more is my worth. I matter to myself and to others. The lower my status, the less my worth. Since I do not matter to others, I do not have their respect, nor do I have any influence.

People in shame-based groups struggle with their position in comparison to others around them. They need to know the pecking order in the group, who is 'on top' and how the rest of the group relates to one another.

The ancient Romans had developed a highly stratified society, believing that everyone had to know their place in relation to everyone else in their social group. It was very important to maintain distinctions. Everyone could not be the same as everyone else. If this was confused, then no one would know whom to respect and whom not to respect. Those with higher status had more power to promote themselves and their families.

Ascribed or achieved status

In many cultures, people experience 'ascribed status' because they are connected to an important family or person. For example, the president of a university is considered a VIP and enjoys special status and honour. So their relatives also appreciate status and privilege because they are connected to the president.

> *People in shame-based groups struggle with their position in comparison to others around them*

In 'achieved status', a person may become a popular athlete or movie star or develop a wealthy business by stepping out of their own comfort zone and taking risks. They take full responsibility for their initiatives, and if they succeed they will gain respect and honour from others.

A new status: belonging to Jesus

When a person becomes a follower of the Messiah, what happens to their status? Many believers experience deep shame from their family when they decide to follow Christ. It is essential that we understand our status as Christians, and secondly, for believers who struggle with shame from their own social group, how they can live with a renewed honour.

We have many privileges as followers of Jesus. We are embraced by the love of God, seated in a place of honour. God lifts up our heads. We become the Creator's VIPs, His special envoys here on earth. We receive new honour and a new status as children of the Heavenly Father.

But often that is not enough. We want special honour from our new social group (the church). At times, a Christian worker sees their position as pastor, director or manager as a means to gain more human status and privilege. This easily leads to suspicion, arguments, and even corruption, clearly not the honour that Christ gives to His people.

The young believers in Rome, Philippi and elsewhere in Asia Minor understood status and honour as expressed in their own social groups. Members in religious or political associations competed for higher status and more honour. For Jews, it came through keeping the Mosaic law.

Now as they began to follow Jesus, as their King, and gathered as a group of believers, what would the culture in this new association look like? Would young believers compete for rank and privilege in their new group as they did in their former associations?

- If a young man, whose father had been a respected general, joined a Messiah group, would he carry special respect because of his 'ascribed' status as the son of a general?
- If a wealthy cloth merchant, who owned a house in Philippi, was leading a group of believers, would she be a 'higher,' more respected follower of Jesus?
- If a devout Jew, known for achieving status as a Hebrew scholar, was convinced that Jesus fulfilled the Old Testament story, would he continue his position?

Would these VIPs demand special respect and status in the new Jesus movement? Or would those who had little status in their former walks of life, struggle to gain status through gaining special position in the group of believers?

Paul had ascribed status, being connected to true Hebrew stock, and relished in his good standing by having faultlessly followed the Jewish law. But now, he rejected both, considering these titles of honour as meaningless. As a follower of Jesus, Paul genuinely, and even viscerally, experienced his new status in the Messiah. True value, privilege and honour lay in the Messiah, belonging to Him and following His way (Phil. 3:2-8).

A new status: serving like Jesus

Shaikh Saadi, the 14th century Persian poet wrote this: "It is the person themselves that gives dignity to a human, not these lovely clothes that are a sign of a human."

A person with higher status often uses symbols to show the public their position and impress others in their group that they are worthy of respect. Titles like Doctor or Professor (or Pastor or Engineer in some cultures) often carry exceptional respect. Special clothes or jewelry, Rolex watches, cushioned furniture, or SUV vehicles for warlords—all communicate status and position of honour.

> *A person with higher status often uses symbols to show their position and impress others in the group*

The ancient Romans relished in such symbols. They wore special clothes, and displayed their status and achievements through statues of themselves or inscriptions that boasted about their feats. They found resourceful ways to show the public that they were indeed noteworthy.

As Jesus proclaimed God's Kingdom and invited disciples to join his group, many expected they would gain honour through this new Messiah movement. Once Jesus would set up His rule, each one of them would receive special privilege and position. The disciples argued among themselves about who had more status (Mark 9:34).

At one point two of Jesus' disciples, James and John, quietly requested that Jesus give them a special position when He started His rule. This would give them more respect and privilege (Mark 10:35-45).

The others were offended. If James and John got more status, it meant that the rest of them would have less status and less respect. They became jealous.

Jesus did not tell the disciples to reject honour and greatness. Rather he told them, "In my kingdom, the way to be first, and have more respect, is to care for other people."

This is Jesus' greatness, who laid aside His honour for the world. It is not ascribed or achieve honour. It is 'serving status', a new way of humility, esteeming others ahead of oneself. This is the highest status and how God's kingdom works.

Jesus redefines status, "the status of belonging to him and of serving others".

To talk about

- In what ways can young believers from shame-based groups genuinely and emotionally experience the privilege and joy of being called children of God?
- We often see humility as spiritually bowing our hearts before Almighty God. Describe humility in terms of social relationships.

The Director: boss or friend? Power-distance and caring

In leadership workshops in Central Asia, we often compare the strengths and weaknesses of an authoritarian (power, position) leader with a people (relational) leader. Normally, the people leader receives a better rating. We appreciate a leader who likes being with their staff, sits down with them for a cup of tea, and relates to them as friends and peers.

But after a few minutes of discussion, someone in the workshop blurts out, "But it won't take long before we will have ripped such a leader into shreds." Or, they say, "If the director is too friendly, their staff won't respect them." For this reason, directors usually distance themselves.

Position with honour

Some cultures naturally resort to a top-down style of leadership. A director is credited with ascribed honour because of their position.

In one leadership workshop at a government institute, the professors wanted me to meet the director first. They led me up a large stairway, down the hall, into a receiving room, and then into a large office, with couches and chairs. At the far end of this great room was an immense desk, with a leather armchair. Rising from behind the desk was a smallish man in a white suit, the President of the college. He greeted me cordially, but I soon wondered, "Does he even know that we're having a leadership seminar today?"

This president had honour. He carried respect, at least outwardly, because of his *title* as 'The President.' But he seemed far off from those he was leading.

This is high power-distance, where the leader remains separate from those they are leading. This distance is both physical and psychological, often expressed by attitude and behaviour. Because the director is 'higher-up', the staff tends to 'look up' (respect) to the director, and the director tends to 'look down' (disrespect) on the staff.

Why distance?

Why would directors naturally distance themselves from the people they lead? These answers were provided by a leadership class in Afghanistan:

- Distance gives a director a sense of significance. He feels good that people have to work to meet him. He is busy with major issues and should not need to relate to petty issues of the community. This would be demeaning to him.
- Distance shelters a director from criticism. He can hide or cover up his shortcomings and failures if he is distant from his staff and clients.
- Distance helps a director keep secrets. He does not need to be accountable or open with the people. This breeds suspicion and more easily leads to corruption.

This means the more separation or distance between a director and staff, the more respect the director receives.[1] In other words, the greater the distance the director maintains from others, the more power lies in their hands.

Here is the question for directors and managers (including pastors, teachers and parents): what distance are you from those you lead?

'Top-down' or 'face-to-face' leader

Consider these scenarios. Which are more effective?

- Should a director give orders or consult with their staff and ask questions?

---

1 See discussion on "power-distance" in Geert Hofstede and Gert Jan Hofstede, *Cultures and Organizations – Software of the Mind; Intercultural Cooperation and Its Importance for Survival* (New York: McGraw-Hill, 2005), 39-72.

- Should students stand up to show respect to their teachers or can they be more casual, like addressing teachers by their first names?
- Should children obey their parents or relate to them as friends?
- Should a manager be a boss or a friend?

In the Christian world, we have an abundance of teaching on servant leadership, with Jesus presented as the Servant of all. In management courses, we emphasise horizontal, 'on-the-floor' leadership, where leaders and managers are in touch with those they lead.

But if honour depends on position, titles and status, and if directors naturally give orders 'from the top', how should we understand 'servant leadership' where a master washed his disciples' feet, sat with servants and bestowed dignity?

> *If honour depends on position, titles and status, how should we understand 'servant leadership'?*

When a director's honour and influence depends on maintaining a distance from the staff, it becomes difficult for him or her to mingle with them and listen to them. As noted above, respect will be lost, and the director may no longer be considered the leader.

Servant leadership does not need to reject top-down patterns or adapt to horizontal, egalitarian ways. The question can be framed differently: How can a top-down director also be a 'people leader' without losing their authority and honour? How can a director maintain their distance and influence, while at the same time developing healthy team relationships?

Caring leadership

It is possible for an authoritarian leader to *care* for their personnel (or church group) and yet carry respect and maintain their own honour.

The United Nations Universal Declaration of Human Rights argues for the "the equal and inalienable rights" of all human beings. Christians believe in the universal value and dignity of every individual because everyone bears the image of God. Islamic theology teaches that humans are *ashraf al-makhluqat*, the noble (great, dignified, valuable) creation.

Directors who understand the worth and value of every person in their sphere of responsibility, will relate to them in that light. They will care for them and give them value.

If a director gives attention and honour to their employees, rather than losing some of their own honour, they will have gained true honour. When a pastor, who thrives on the privilege of leading his or her flock, moves 'downward' in order to sit with them, listen to their stories and seek to understand their issues, they will not lose but gain respect. In both cases, the director or pastor has gained honour and respect in the eyes of others.

> *When a pastor moves downward in order to sit with their flock, they will not lose but gain respect*

Entering the story

When someone thinks about us, we feel encouraged and honoured. Afghans say, "That person entered my story." Many people die emotionally and spiritually because they feel, "no one thinks about me, no one cares about me."

The word *story* is an interesting way to express how someone cares for another person. My 'story' refers to my experiences, failures and successes. When someone doesn't care for me, I feel dishonoured by that person, as if that person has slighted me. But when someone does care for me, I experience value and inner joy. They have entered my story.

This is what God has done. He entered the 'human story' in the Messiah. As His followers, we are called to continue the same mindset as our Master: to enter the stories of other people.

Thinking of others' welfare was far from the minds of Roman citizens. The Roman satirist Lucian wrote, "[the elite] not only have never shared with us, but never deign even to notice ordinary people."[2] Such humility, in the sense of caring for others, was no virtue in ancient Roman or Greek ethics.

However, Paul urges the believers in Philippi to do just that: to be genuinely interested in others, to esteem and honour them.

> *Do nothing out of selfish ambition or vain conceit. Rather, in humility value others above yourselves, not looking to your own interests but each of you to the interests of the others. Your attitude should be the same as that of Christ Jesus (Philippians 2:3-4).*

This is how we honour the Messiah: when we show *interest* in others. Paul speaks of Timothy, caring for Christ because he cared for others.

> *I have no one else like [Timothy], who will show genuine concern for your welfare. For everyone looks out for their own interests, not those of Jesus Christ (Philippians 2:20-21).*

When a director looks at me and asks, "How are you?" as more than a greeting, I sense that they really want to hear from me and learn from my experiences. They want to enter my story when they give me their ear. They honour me by caring for my story.

To talk about

- As a leader or a manager, how can you honour others? How can you enter their stories?
- Think of five specific ways in which an organisational director can really care for their personnel.

---

2   Quoted in Hellerman, J. *Embracing Shared Ministry: Power and Status in the Early Church and Why It Matters Today*, Kriegel Ministry, 2013, 38

The Pastor: patronage and the honour game

BEING an honourable leader means more than carrying respect. People honour their leader by following them. In order for a leader to maintain his or her honour, they need to ensure that people follow them. So how should he or she maintain their loyalty? Should it be by control of the people? And if so, how much control should be exercised? How should pastors express authority or implement God's will (which may simply be the pastor's will) to those in their flock?

Every culture has its own understanding of how authority relates to leadership. Traditionally, we learn about authority from our fathers, from the way fathers relate to their wife, children and neighbours. We then continue these patterns in our own lives.

Which is the 'better' example?

The 'equal' father/husband	The 'ruling' father/husband
• Wife is equal, a friend	• Wife must submit and obey
• Discipline: talks with children	• Disciplines, orders children
• Children don't fear him	• Children respect from fear
• Sees himself as partner with wife	• Sees himself as provider and protector
• Peace through harmony	• Peace through uniformity or conformity
• Encourages independence in children	• Family is dependent
• Elders are on their own	• Elders are cared for by children

As we look at these two lists of characteristics, can we say which list is more biblical or more Christian? A person from a culture where relationships are more egalitarian will likely prefer the 'equal father/husband', and a person from a 'high-position' culture, may prefer the 'ruling father/husband' list. Which is the better model for a pastor? Before considering this question, let us look at the patron-client system.

Patron-client relationships

> Asheel works as a labourer for a construction company. He has six children and a seventh is on the way. His oldest son is old enough to get married, and so he needs to find a bride for him. His youngest daughter is very ill and they need a specialist for her kidney problem. But Asheel has no money. He tells his pastor, "I'm helpless; I don't know what to do. I've asked everyone I know for a loan, but no one is helping."

It is as if Asheel is locked in a dark room and desperate to find a way out, but all doors are closed. He needs to have connection, to find someone who will ensure protection, provision and security for him and his family. Asheel needs a patron. So his question is: "Who do I know ... maybe my pastor?"

The patronage system has always been an important means of acquiring goods and securities

Many traditional societies are built on patron-client relationships. The ancient Roman philosopher Seneca said, "The practice of patronage constitutes the chief bond of human society".[3]

Since time immemorial, the patronage system has been an important means of acquiring goods and securities in life. But it is much more than an economic framework. It is the way to honour, both for the patron and for the clients.

---

3 Cited in David deSilva, *Honour, Patronage, Kinship and Purity: Unlocking New Testament Culture* (Intervarsity Press, 2000), 96.

The patron

A patron is like a father. In fact, the English word 'father' comes from the Latin word, *pater*. The patron, almost always male, becomes like a father-figure for his clients.

A patron is someone with means and power. He has connections to others with even more means and power. Needy people connect to a patron who will provide for them. From the perspective of the patron, the more loyal clients (followers) he has, the more honour he receives. So the patron looks for people whom he can serve and who will be loyal to him.

In order for the patron to ensure this loyalty, he must be seen to be generous, like a benefactor who provides for people's needs—material or non-material. As he provides for others, they in turn boast about him and spread his fame to others.

Clients

The word 'client' comes from the Latin term *cluens* meaning, 'to heed, to hear, or to obey'. It used to refer to people who experienced genuine needs in life, and therefore lived under the protection or guarantee of a provider, someone who was like a parent for them.

Like our example of Asheel, a client looks for support, a guarantor or a patron. When he finds a good patron, the client will follow him and repay the patron with honour, loyalty and obedience. He will serve the patron faithfully and be committed to the patron. As the patron graces him with more support, the client spreads the patron's fame. Through this public praise, the patron's honour increases.

Patronage can be a wonderful system of mutual support. People from traditional societies have not had systems of health-care, job security, or government education. They normally gain security and worth in life, through their connections to those with value and worth. So, 'who you know' becomes extremely significant.

The caring pastor/patron

As one who should care and watch for the sheep and ensure their protection from dangers (see Acts 20:28), a pastor indeed has a divine calling to be a godly patron for his or her congregation. But to what extent?

The Scriptural teaching is clear: feed the flock, care for them, teach and build them up. We know these principles well. Many pastors selflessly sacrifice their time and energy for the sake of the flock. But if a pastor's personal honour and good name depends on a loyal, obedient church, how should they relate to individual members in their needs?

The controlling pastor/patron

Should a pastor be like a 'ruling father' who sets out to control his people? Since they are under his or her care and since they provide him or her with honour, they cannot afford to lose them. They must provide for the 'flock' in order to 'keep' them.

As a patron, the pastor sees himself or herself as holding the treasure of spiritual (and material) resources which he or she needs to impart to the flock. Furthermore, he or she will tend to make decisions unilaterally without consulting others, as patrons in traditional cultures would do without listening to or negotiating with their clients.

What happens if the patron-pastor is not able to provide the type of support that the people request, or if a member in the church finds a better pastor? Or if the members are not as loyal as the pastor expects they should be?

Should the pastor rebuke them? Do they resort to force, threats or insults in order to make sure they stay with them? Often the relationship between a pastor and a young church can turn sour because the new believers feel that their pastor tries to rule them and actually does not care for them.

Jesus: another model of patron

Jesus rebuked the religious leaders of his day for their efforts to be controlling fathers and honour-seeking patrons. He told his disciples:

> *But you are not to be called 'Rabbi,' for you have one Teacher, and you are all brothers. And do not call anyone on earth 'father,' for you have one Father, and he is in heaven. Nor are you to be called instructors, for you have one Instructor, the Messiah. The greatest among you will be your servant. For those who exalt themselves will be humbled, and those who humble themselves will be exalted (Matthew 23:8-12).*

When His own disciples argued among themselves as to who was the more honourable and powerful among them, Jesus strongly rebuked them:

> *The kings of the Gentiles lord it over them; and those who exercise authority over them call themselves Benefactors. But you are not to be like that. Instead, the greatest among you should be like the youngest, and the one who rules like the one who serves (Luke 22:24).*

Worldly leaders normally control people in two ways:

- by force, using threats and military power
- by granting benefits: money, patronage, or gifts in kind

Jesus says to every pastor, "You are not to lead or pastor as benefactor." This seems odd. A benefactor is one who does good to others. Indeed, a pastor should care for his church, but the benefits (spiritual or material) should *not* be used as leverage to control the people. After Jesus fed the five thousand, he taught the crowd that he was the true bread of life. As a result, many left him. He then asked his disciples if they too wanted to leave him (John 6:67).

The pastor's true honour comes not from controlling his flock, but as Jesus says, by serving others. And the fundamental characteristic in serving is *humility*. The humble patron is a pastor who seeks God's honour and secondly, the church's honour. For the patron-pastor, the way up is to step down, like our Messiah, so that the church can step up.

To talk about
- Discuss what type of 'father' or 'patron' role a pastor should have in their church.
- What are some dangers of a pastor if he becomes too much like a father for his church?

The Teacher: empowerment and success

After leading a small media team for many years, Basir was ready to retire. However, he cared for the ministry and wanted to see it continue. He committed himself to building a new team and so continued his work for two more years. After listening to others, he selected a young couple and threw himself into seeing them grow in faith and media skills so they could replace him. He spent time with them, advised them and began to organise and transfer his resources to them. Two years later, when the larger team came together for reporting time, he pulled back, "Now it is time for the younger couple to present the report. It is my joy to see them take over this team."

In the current vocabulary of development and aid, a popular term is 'capacity building'. In church life we call it discipleship. Jesus said, "Make disciples ... teach them what I have taught you." (Matthew 28:19-20) Paul says much the same, "Entrust these things to reliable persons, who will teach others." (2 Timothy 2:2)

No society can develop if we do not train the younger generation. Every good teacher knows they must train others in skills, character and Bible knowledge, especially younger persons, so that God's Kingdom will continue to grow.

But often problems develop. A teacher notices that a student or colleague performs better or grows stronger in various capacities. Suddenly they are seized by worry: "What if that person becomes more successful than I am? My colleague will get more credit!" Without realising it, a destructive spirit of jealousy takes root in the teacher's heart. And because of this jealousy, the teacher holds back some information and retards the development process.

From jealousy to killing

We see this spirit in Adam's son, Cain. Although Cain was the older brother, God recognised Abel's offering. Cain felt dishonoured, his "face was downcast" (Genesis 4:5). God gave him a chance to restore face, but Cain's envy at his brother was deep. He could not tolerate his brother's honour (success), and so he rose up and killed him, removing his rival and hoping to restore his 'lost' honour.

This is jealousy. We envy other people's positions, privileges and promotions. When someone else receives recognition or honour, we feel hurt. When someone else gets more credit than we do, we feel they have stolen our credit.

> *When someone gets more credit than we do, we feel they have stolen our credit*

The ancient Greeks described envy as an emotional or even physical pain when a person sees someone else with good fortune.

James discusses how dangerous envy is. It leads to chaos and evil.

> *If you harbour bitter envy and selfish ambition in your hearts, do not boast about it or deny the truth. Such 'wisdom' does not come down from heaven but is earthly, unspiritual, demonic. For where you have envy and selfish ambition, there you find disorder and every evil practice (James 3:13-16).*

Directors, teachers, and managers who harbour envy will not lead or teach well.

How is envy expressed?

When we envy another person's success, we express it in various ways:

- We tend to ignore that person. Since it is so hard to appreciate another's success, it is better not to notice them. We apply the principle 'out of sight, out of mind'.

- We boast of our own (real or unreal) successes. We want others to notice *us*, and so we elevate ourselves, trying to make a name for ourselves by talking about what we have done.
- We dishonour others with gossip and slander. The logic goes: if others are lowered, then we will appear higher.
- We develop a spirit of competition. Healthy competition can energise us to improve and work harder. However, an excessive spirit of competition easily breeds "disorder and every evil practice."

Envy can lead to mistrust. A teacher suspects that a colleague is trying to make a show for themselves. And so when they come together, each is envious of the other, each suspecting the other of a hidden agenda. Friendships die. The worst result is what Cain did: remove the competition by killing it.

If envy is pain at another's gain, it robs us of joy and delight in others.

From envy to the evil eye

Envy starts by *seeing* another's success.[4] This hurts us. We express (exhale) this pain through our eyes again—the envious look. Through the eyes we wish evil or cast pain towards others. We curse them. That is why the evil eye lurks everywhere, because envy lies hidden in all our hearts.

We are compelled to guard against the evil eye, our own as well as that of others. Daily life becomes very complicated, with constant efforts to stop everybody from being envious of everybody else. Societies use various fetishes and amulets as special instruments to ward off the evil eye.

We come back to the key question: can we overcome the malaise of jealousy that lurks in our hearts, or must we live with this pain?

---

4 The word 'envy' comes from the Latin word *in+vidia*, meaning to 'look over' with a view to control or destroy.

Overcoming envy

Self-awareness

Envy starts when I see others becoming successful. When I recognise the pain of jealousy taking root in my heart, I should address this feeling. I acknowledge the emotion of jealousy and make an inner covenant that I will not allow this spirit to ruin my peace and destroy my relationship with others.

Self-confidence

When I am jealous, it means that I am not secure within myself. Yet everyone is a unique individual with distinct qualities. As I appreciate and practise the gifts God has given me, I develop a healthy self-confidence, doing well the things I am capable of doing, instead of wishing to be like others.

The big picture: win-win

When I see another person's success against my own success, I have very small vision. When I see the bigger picture of God's Kingdom, I look beyond myself, not at *who* is successful (or *who* receives honour).

This is your honour

A great music teacher is the one whose students outdo her in music. A parent wishes their children to become more successful than them. A great leader is delighted when they are able to help others flourish. Others' success becomes the leader's honour and success.

A Persian poem says, "When others flourish, I flourish; I enjoy the joy of others." This is like Paul's words, "rejoice with those who rejoice." (Romans 12:15)

Sow and reap

I can keep information and power to myself, excluding others from growth opportunities and simply taking credit for myself. As a result, information and power stays with me, limited to my own capacity. As I hold power to myself, all of us stagnate. But as we sow and spread our strengths to others, we reap a harvest, and with the harvest comes joy. The more we sow, the more we reap.

From envy to God's generosity

The outgoing nature of God

One of the greatest failures of God's people in the Old Testament was their focus on the top line of the Abrahamic covenant, that God would bless *them*. They ignored the bottom line: that they were to be a blessing to *all*.

God's nature works in two directions. He draws people to Himself, but He also goes out of Himself into the world. God is a sending, giving God. Jesus models this by expending Himself for others. He then says to His disciples, "as the Father sent me [to others], so send I you [to others]" (John 20:21).

We too are sent to others. This shows people what God is like. The power of the Spirit within us must propel us outward to serve and bless others. It can only be this way. We cannot simply receive grace and blessing. If we do, the flow of grace will stop.

See and be moved with compassion

When the Messiah *saw* the crowds, he was moved with compassion and served the people (Matthew 9:36). In the great story of the Good Samaritan, two religious officials saw the needy man, but ignored him. When the Samaritan *saw* him, he took pity on him (Luke 10:33). In the greatest story of the gospels, when the young, needy son was still afar off, his father *saw* him, was filled with compassion and ran to him.

In short, this is God's story. God *sees* our condition, He is moved with compassion. Christian teachers, leaders, directors can do no less. We will overcome the eye of envy when we see others and are moved with compassion for them.

To talk about
- In what ways have you experienced envy and jealousy?
- How can we develop the grace to "rejoice with those who rejoice"?

The Family: honourable and happy homes

A high view of family

Grandfather walks with his three grandchildren to the market and buys each one of them an ice-cream. The children adore Grandfather. He is like a loving king to them. And their father, although he is 40 years old, continues to respect and even obey his 65-year-old father, who is long retired.

THREE generations living in one home—grandparents, parents and children. Grandfather enjoys his old age, not because he is productive and useful in the marketplace, but because of the honour he receives from his married children and young grandchildren. He carries tremendous respect as well as influence, even at an old age.

Fathers rule

In many traditional societies, the parents (and sometimes grandparents) decide on a child's future, career, and selection of spouse. The sons normally continue their father's trade. Their first duty is to bring honour to their father. A father says to his child, "Whatever you do, make sure you keep the family name!"

But in modern, urban settings, this family expectation clashes with other values. Children want more freedom. They want to decide on their lives for themselves.

In the Bollywood movie, *Kubbi Khushi, Kubbi Gham*, a proud father of a wealthy family business bans his son from the family because the son has shamed them by marrying outside the family class. The family unit is shattered. Ten years later, the heart-broken wife says to her husband,

> *You know how mother always says that a husband is god. No matter what he says. No matter what he thinks. He is always right. ... But look at the mess. Our family is shattered. Then how does a husband become god? My husband is just a husband, not god.*

Considering a husband as a god may sound extreme, but is a husband or father always right? While we are commanded to honour our fathers, should a father have the right to *rule* his family? How should a father relate to his family, to his wife and children?

Strong fathers — secure families

We need security in our homes. Usually a multi-generational family with an authoritarian father appears stable. The children give honour to the father so he can hold his head high in the community. As he ages, the children become his pension; they are the security for the parents. Hence, families need to stay together. Their future security depends on it. Western cultures have insurances and pensions, but in most cultures of the Global South, this security is provided by the family.

Although the traditional extended family provides tremendous stability, we need to ask: is this type of family a happy one? If it is stable, at what expense?

Angry fathers — unhappy families

Many short story writers and film producers from the Global South have reflected on another side of the 'secure family.' From their stories, as well as personal experiences, we often hear, "I don't have any happy memories of my father." One Afghan writer profiles an angry father who neglects to take care of the walls around their house, but constantly barks at his family and fights with their neighbour. Eventually the walls crumble, and to everyone's horror, one child lies buried underneath the wall. The walls, as well as the father's belligerent spirit, silenced the child.

Paul emphasises that children must obey their parents. This brings honour to the family. But then he addresses fathers, "Fathers, do not exasperate your children; instead bring them up in the training and instruction of the Lord" (Ephesians 6:3).

Do your children appreciate you and enjoy being with you, or are they afraid of you? Do you ask them about their day in school, and listen to them—not out of suspicion, as if they've done something wrong, but because you are genuinely interested in them?

When fathers care for their children by talking with them and taking interest in their lives, the home is not only security for the future, but becomes a place of joy and peace.

Distant husbands — unhappy marriages

I doubt if there is a culture anywhere in the world that does not celebrate the wedding day. Yet Pashtun women speak of the wedding day as the day when sadness entered their lives.[5] While 'getting married' is an obsession in most Asian societies, one well-known Iranian author describes marriage in this way:

> Most marriages in our country are unsuccessful. Two individuals with two different backgrounds, education, and customs have to endure one another for a lifetime. Well, this very tolerance creates hatred.[6]

Although the marriage relationship provides a secure and honourable base for child-bearing and child-rearing, it should also provide companionship for the parents. Of course the husband-wife relationship

---

5 Benedicte Grima, *The Performance of Emotion among Paxtun Women* (Oxford University Press, 1993), 52-57. Grima argues in her study that 'sadness' is a woman's honour in Pashtun society.
6 Milani, Farzaneh. "Power, Prudence, and Print: Censorship and Simin Daneshvar," *Iranian Studies Journal of the Society for Iranian Studies* Vol. XVIII, Nos. 2-4 (Spring-Autumn 1985): p. 340.

varies from culture to culture as well as from home to home. However, the view that "a man's wife is his honour" (an Arab proverb) links the woman's behaviour to the husband's reputation, which then tends to create a chasm within the marriage relationship, as if the husband and wife live in different worlds. To this day, many 'honourable' husbands see it as below their dignity to express companionship and emotional intimacy with their spouse. Ironically, the husband must 'dishonour' his wife, by distancing himself from her, in order to receive honour in public.

> *The challenge for Christian families is to bring honour and happiness together in the home*

Modern literature from the Global South generally disparages the traditional view of marriage because, as they express it, men live by a different standard than the demands they place on the women in their household. Yet both spouses crave intimacy and companionship. The challenge for Christian families is to bring honour and happiness together in the home.

Responses

We do not want to emulate Western ways with their soaring divorce rates, where many couples ignore the marriage covenant. We also reject the restrictive responses of conservative religion where women must be covered (physically and emotionally), as well as the machismo ways of Latino culture, where men often consider sexual conquest as 'manly'.

Four words: cling, honour, leave, continue

The amazing words given for the first married couple, "to leave and **cling**" (Genesis 2:24), is foundational to an honourable husband-wife relationship. Husbands and wives must covenant their relationship as priority over and exclusive to, yet within the context of, other relationships.

The first positive *mitzvah* (command) from the Ten Laws of God, "**Honour** your father and mother," is repeated by Jesus and Paul. This is a call to honour the family unit and keep it central.

However, Jesus' teaching also runs counter to the family. He told his followers to **leave** the family. This is a daunting challenge. Jesus calls followers to seek first the family of God. When the father rules the family, this kingdom stands juxtaposed to God's Kingdom. Our loyalty must be to our Lord.[7]

But then again, Paul honours his younger colleague Timothy, whose grandmother and mother passed on the faith to their son and grandson. They **continued** the family line. We should esteem the multi-generational family cluster, for it is the family group that provides the needed security and continuity in a chaotic world.

The family as place of serving

In traditional cultures, couples were much more connected with relatives and their communities. As societies have urbanised, marriage has become more private and less attached to community. However, when the marriage relationship is too private and focused on itself, it becomes difficult to sustain itself, "too separate and too little to do."[8]

The family unit should be a peaceful haven, a place of security, but not an end in itself. Rather, through the family we serve those around us. The family cluster becomes a serving base for relatives and the community around it.

---

7 I believe the proverbial teaching, "God first, family second, ministry third," is over-stated and even misused. We must seek God and His Kingdom first, and from this centre flow the many spheres of life, including family, work and other relationships.

8 Denis Hiebert, *Sweet Surrender: How Cultural Mandates Shape Christian Marriage* (Cascade Books, 2013), 49.

To talk about

- *Extended family*: Can you focus on the small tri-unit of father-mother-children in the context of the larger family of grandparents and relatives?
- *Hospitality*: What can you do to make your home a centre of joy for others, and include relatives, neighbours and friends around the dinner table?
- *Spouses*: What if you spent thirty minutes a day talking together, asking each other about the day? What would happen if you as a husband intentionally listened to your wife, or you as a wife genuinely showed interest in your husband?
- *Anger and children*: In what ways do parents exasperate or frustrate their children?

Conclusion

When we experience the new status of belonging to the Messiah, we no longer need to compete for honour. We carry a new name. We live with different values, seeing the world and people around us differently. Indeed, *all* things have been made new. We no longer need to struggle to overcome shame, because the Messiah carried our shame.

We are able to truly honour and value others, as God has honoured us in the Messiah.

Honour does not come simply as we 'rise to the top', but as we *care* for others. Honour need not be based on how many people follow us, but rather on the privilege to bless others in a spirit of humility. While we naturally crave credit for ourselves, our vision expands when we experience transformed honour, so that we can rejoice with the success of others.

Perhaps the greatest challenge remains in the family relationship. When husbands and wives cling to each other, when we honour and continue the family unit yet acknowledge God's family as the highest priority, this should result in joy and companionship in the home.

Some helpful resources

Chris Flanders, *About Face: Rethinking Face for 21st Century Mission* (2011) American Society of Missiology Monograph (Book 9), Wipf and Stock. An anthropological study of how the Gospel relates to the honour culture of Thailand.

Jayson Georges, *The 3-D Gospel* (2014) Timē Press. An easy-to-read comparison of guilt-innocence, power-fear and honour-shame orientations.

Jayson Georges, "The Good News for Honor-Shame Cultures: Uncovering a core aspect of God's mission", *Lausanne Global Analysis*, 6:2, March 2017. https://www.lausanne.org/content/lga/2017-03/the-good-news-for-honor-shame-cultures

Joseph Hellerman, *Embracing Shared Ministry: Power and Status in the Early Church and Why it Matters Today* (2013) Kriegel Ministry. A cultural and biblical study on Philippians, exploring how the Christian way countered ancient Roman cultural patterns.

Werner Mischke, *The Global Gospel: Achieving Missional Impact in Our Multicultural World* (2014) Mission ONE. A missiological discussion on how the Gospel uncovers the blind spot about honour/shame in Western theology—why we have it, why it matters for world evangelisation, and what to do about it.

Jackson Wu, *Saving God's Face: A Chinese Contextualization of Salvation through Honor and Shame* (2013) EMS Dissertation Series, William Carey International University Press. A theological study in Scripture and Chinese cultures.

www.honorshame.com: An interactive on-line training on honour-shame thought.

Micah is a global network and movement of Christian organisations and individuals, committed to integral mission as expressed through their response in ministries including relief, rehabilitation, development, creation care, justice, and peacemaking.

Established in 2001, Micah now has over 750 members in 96 countries.

Our vision inspires us towards the realisation of communities living life in all its fullness, free from extreme poverty, injustice or conflict. Grounded in the Gospel, and becoming agents of change in our communities, we work to do this in three ways:

- Being a catalyst for transforming mission through the promotion of integral mission
- Working as a movement towards a united response to advocating for poverty reduction, justice, equality, reconciliation, safety and well-being for all
- Having fellowship as a network, providing a platform for shared learning, corporate reflection and action, and facilitation of an information provision hub

Our motivating call to action is captured in Micah 6:8:

> What does the LORD require of you? To act justly, and to love mercy, and to walk humbly with your God.

Find us at http://www.micahglobal.org